BRAIN GAME **TREASURE HUNTS**

PYRAMID PUZZLES

Thanks to the creative team:
Senior Editor: Alice Peebles
Designer: www.collaborate.agency

Hungry Tomato™
A division of Lerner Publishing Group, Inc.
241 First Avenue North
Minneapolis, MN 55401 USA

For reading levels and more information, look up this title at www.lernerbooks.com.

Main body text set in Eurostile Regular 11/11.5.
Typeface provided by Microsoft.

Library of Congress Cataloging-in-Publication Data
Names: Moore, Gareth, 1975– author.
Title: Pyramid puzzles / by Dr. Gareth Moore
Description: Minneapolis : Hungry Tomato, [2016] | Series: Brain game treasure hunts | Audience: Ages 8–12. | Audience: Grades 4 to 6.
Identifiers: LCCN 2015050910 (print) | LCCN 2016002261 (ebook) | ISBN 9781512406221 (lb : alk. paper) | ISBN 9781512411768 (pb : alk. paper) | ISBN 9781512409284 (eb pdf)
Subjects: LCSH: Puzzles—Juvenile literature. | Logic puzzles—Juvenile literature. | Pyramids—Juvenile literature. | Picture puzzles—Juvenile literature.
Classification: LCC GV1493 .M5567 2016 (print) | LCC GV1493 (ebook) | DDC 793.8—dc23

LC record available at http://lccn.loc.gov/2015050910

Manufactured in the United States of America
1-39295-21132-5/10/2016

BRAIN GAME TREASURE HUNTS

PYRAMID PUZZLES

by Dr. Gareth Moore

Minneapolis

CONTENTS

Pictures like this one are called *hieroglyphs*. The ancient Egyptians used hieroglyphs to represent words. In this book, whenever you see the word *hieroglyph*, it is referring to an individual picture, like this one.

PYRAMID PUZZLES INTRODUCTION

You're in Egypt, the land of the pharaohs, and you are just beginning a visit to a recently discovered ancient pyramid.

The wind is stirring up a sandstorm outside, so you are glad to get inside the pyramid, where you find yourself all alone. The incredibly well-preserved hieroglyphs inside the pyramid are so colorful that you don't notice the sand piling up at the entrance—until it is too late, and you are trapped inside!

Welcome! This is a special kind of book. It contains a story with lots of puzzles, but these puzzles don't always tell you exactly what to do—they provide only a certain amount of information, and then it's up to you to work out what to do and how to solve them!

If you get stuck, use the hints provided. They are an important part of each puzzle, and you will need them for at least a few puzzles. Read them one at a time and only go back for more if you are still stuck! They are meant to help you rather than solve the whole puzzle.

LET THERE BE LIGHT

It's pretty dark now that the entrance is sealed. You are relieved to find some unlit torches and holders on the wall to fit them into.

INSTALLING TORCHES

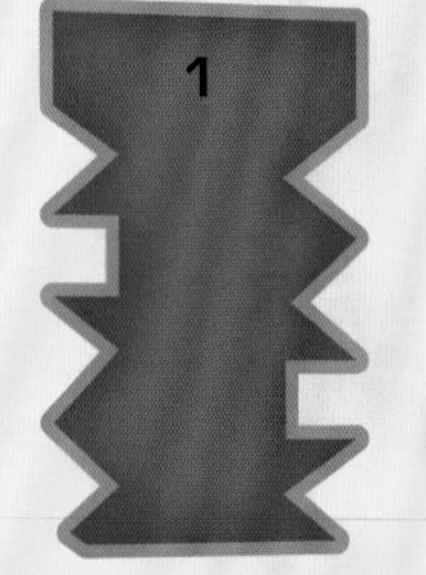

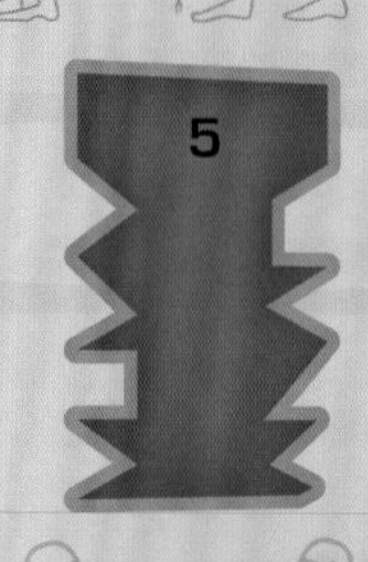

There are five holders on the wall, shown above, and five movable torches that look like this:

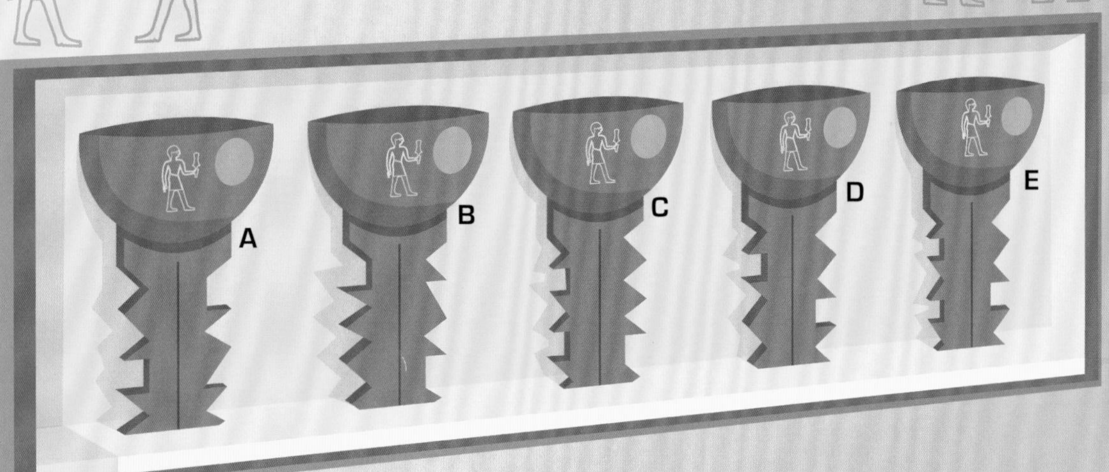

In the picture above, the wall holders have been numbered 1 to 5, and the torches, labeled with letters A to E. Each torch will fit into just one of the holders, but can you work out which goes where?

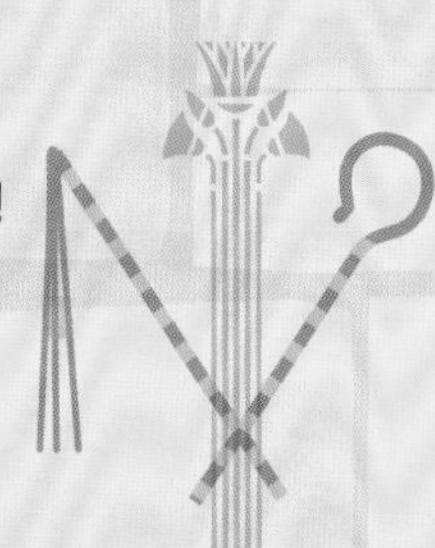

You install the torches in their holders, but now you need to light them!

You look around and find some matches, which are set out in patterns with handwritten instructions alongside them, as shown below.

LIGHTING THE WAY

Can you move two matches to end up with exactly two triangles? All the matches must be used by the two triangles—no leftover or overlapping matches are allowed.

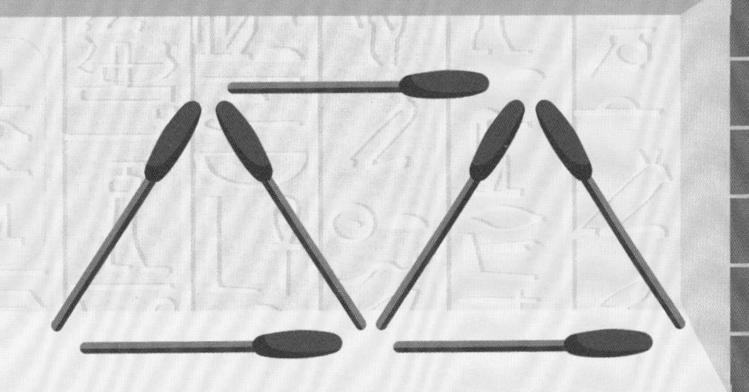

It appears that someone who enjoys puzzles has been here recently!

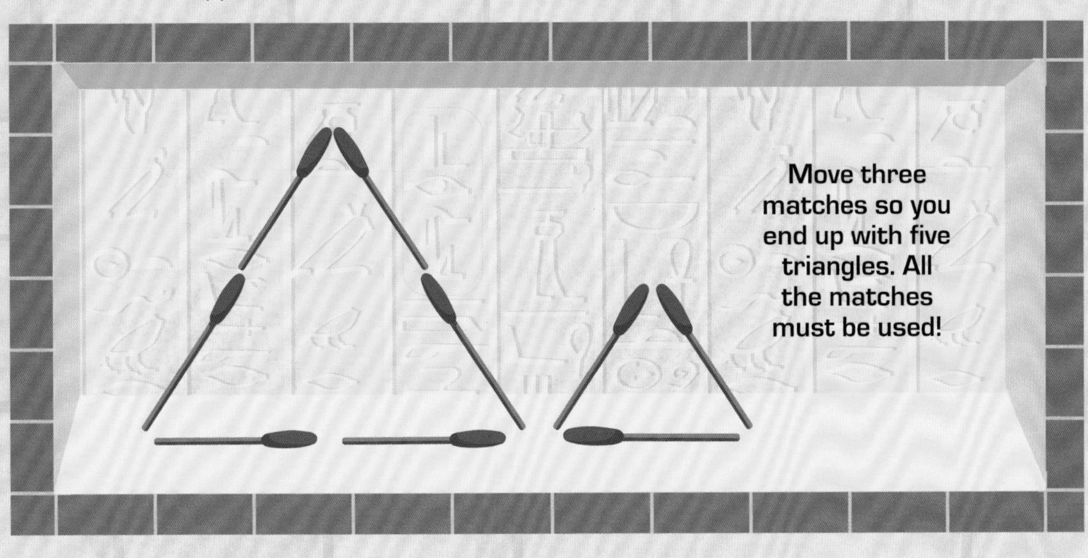

Move three matches so you end up with five triangles. All the matches must be used!

Can you solve these two matchstick puzzles? Instead of matches, use pencils, pens, straws, or any other long, thin objects to try them out.

Once you finish, you light the torches and continue to explore.

A HIEROGLYPH MYSTERY

You enter a chamber that contains the following panel with hieroglyphs and arrows as well as the maze below.

Each of the different hieroglyphs represents a different number from 1 to 6—so it's a code to crack.

ACROSS THE TILED FLOOR

Work out the value of each hieroglyph so that when you begin at the START tile and follow the directions, you reach the EXIT tile without moving onto or over any of the snake tiles!

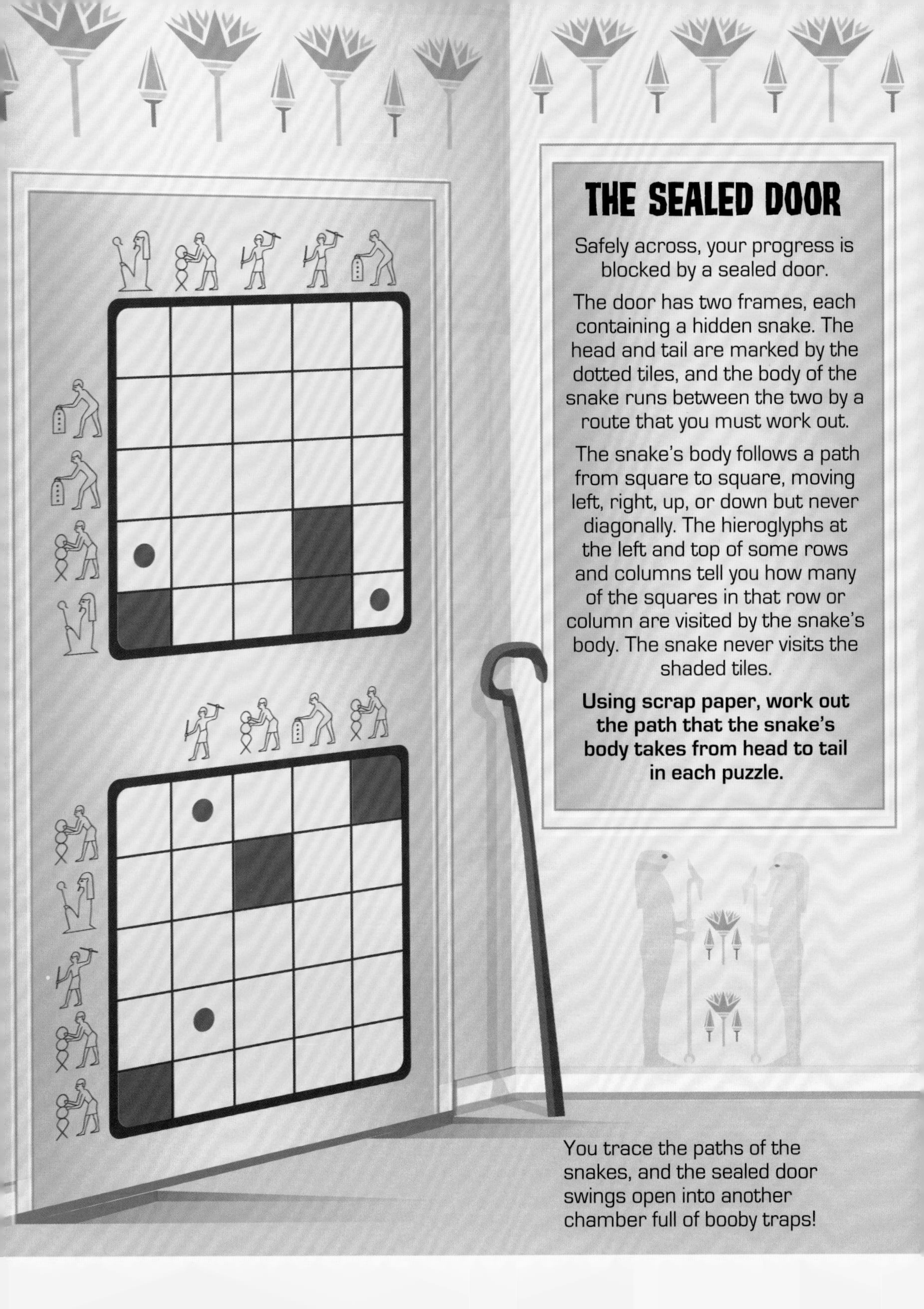

THE SEALED DOOR

Safely across, your progress is blocked by a sealed door.

The door has two frames, each containing a hidden snake. The head and tail are marked by the dotted tiles, and the body of the snake runs between the two by a route that you must work out.

The snake's body follows a path from square to square, moving left, right, up, or down but never diagonally. The hieroglyphs at the left and top of some rows and columns tell you how many of the squares in that row or column are visited by the snake's body. The snake never visits the shaded tiles.

Using scrap paper, work out the path that the snake's body takes from head to tail in each puzzle.

You trace the paths of the snakes, and the sealed door swings open into another chamber full of booby traps!

NUMBERED DOORS

This chamber has three exits, each marked with three numbers. There are traps all over the room, and each time the traps fire, one arrow will hit each of the doors.

THE ROOM OF ARROWS

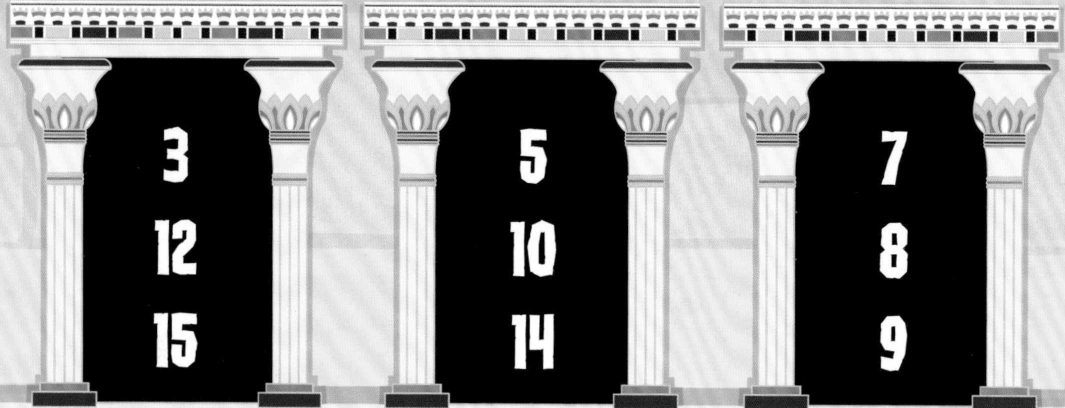

The room also contains four canopic jars, shown below, each with a different number on it. When the arrows fire, the three numbers they hit—one on each door—always add up to one of the values on the jars.

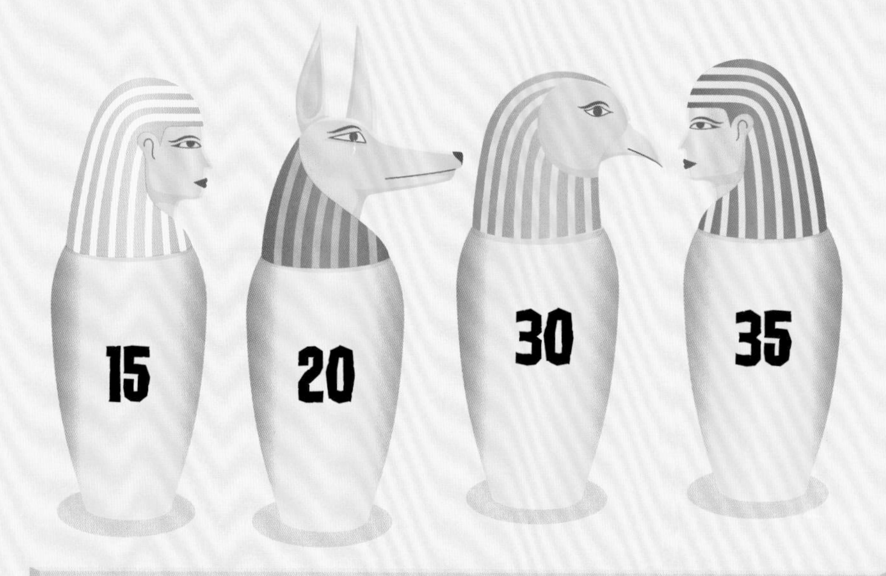

For each number on a canopic jar you can make the same total by picking one number from each door. For example, 15 = 3 + 5 + 7.
Find the correct value from each door to make the total on each jar.

Using your knowledge of where the arrows will fire, you safely cross the room.

You enter a small chamber, and your eye is immediately drawn to a partially complete grid of tiles laid out on the sandy floor.

ARROW HIEROGLYPHS

Diagonally across the grid is a line in the sand, marking four empty spaces where tiles can fit. Beside the grid is a sign:

IF I POINT AT YOU, THEN I'M GREATER THAN YOU, SO WHICH FOUR TILES SHOULD YOU PLACE ON THE LINE?

There is also a set of eight loose tiles that you can pick up and move across onto the grid. They look like this:

As the sign says, the arrows point at hieroglyphs with smaller values. Using this information, can you work out which four loose tiles should fit into the empty spaces marked by the line in the sand?

You place the four missing tiles, and suddenly a hidden door swings open, revealing what appears to be a mummy's burial chamber!

THE MUMMY'S CHAMBER

In the mummy's chamber, you find an arrangement of nine canopic jars. They are laid out in a 3×3 grid, as viewed from above on the page below. The door of the mummy's casket swings open and reveals instructions for two puzzle tasks to solve.

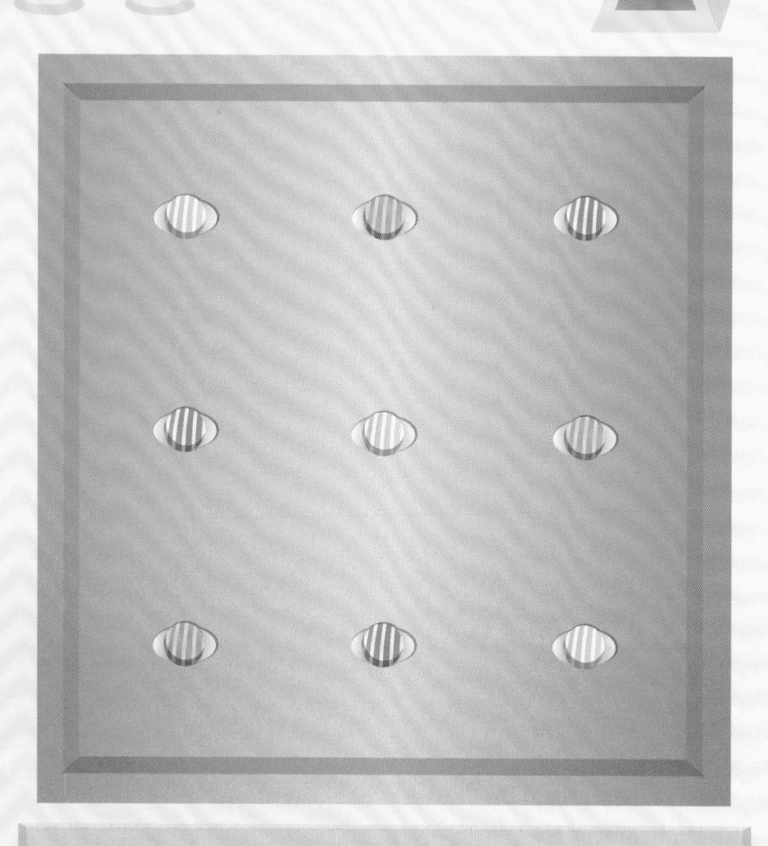

Your first task is to join the jars. You need to find a way to draw a single continuous path that visits all nine jars but is made up of only *FOUR* straight lines. It would be easy with five lines, but four is much harder!

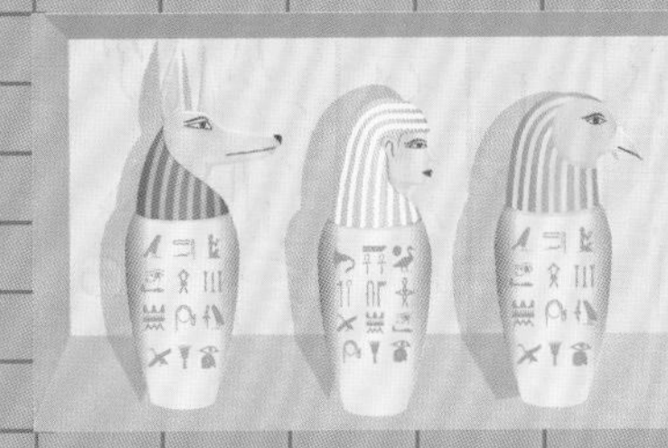

You know canopic jars were used to store organs from mummies, but thankfully these are empty!

The second task is very precise and challenges you to draw *THREE* squares so that you end up with nine separate areas. Each area must have exactly one jar inside it.

You draw lines in the sand to indicate both the path and the three required squares. As you complete these, the sand starts to fall away, revealing a hidden room below.

PYRAMID PILES

Sliding down into the room below, you find two pyramid-shaped piles of blocks. They look like this:

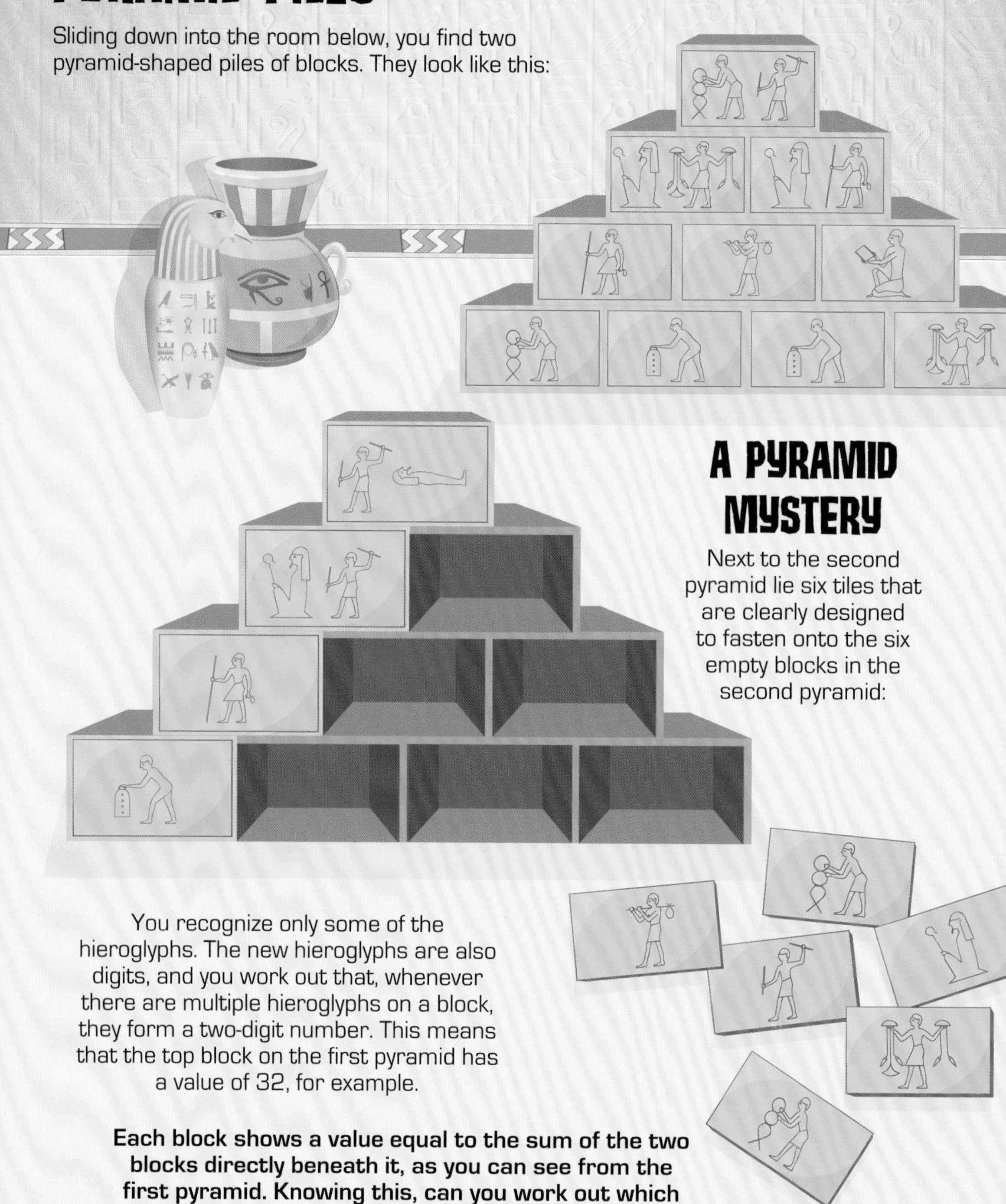

A PYRAMID MYSTERY

Next to the second pyramid lie six tiles that are clearly designed to fasten onto the six empty blocks in the second pyramid:

You recognize only some of the hieroglyphs. The new hieroglyphs are also digits, and you work out that, whenever there are multiple hieroglyphs on a block, they form a two-digit number. This means that the top block on the first pyramid has a value of 32, for example.

Each block shows a value equal to the sum of the two blocks directly beneath it, as you can see from the first pyramid. Knowing this, can you work out which empty block each of the six loose tiles fits onto?

A SECRET PANEL

When you complete the pyramid, a panel appears that shows three puzzles, each made up of a number of tiles. At the top-left of the panel are eighteen movable dividers, along with six dividers that have already been placed into the top puzzle.

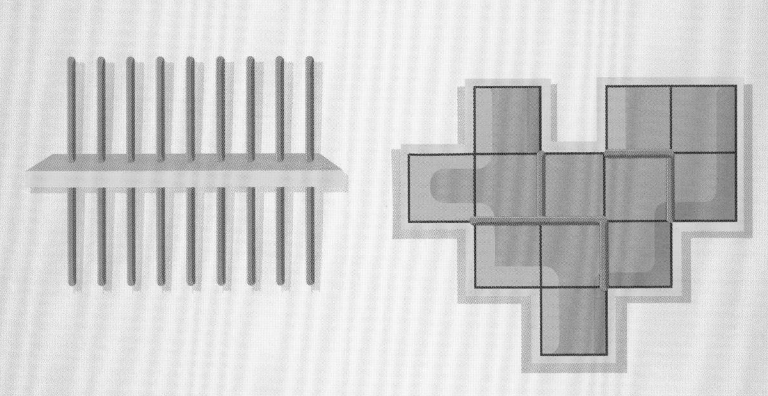

Looking at the top puzzle more closely, you see that the dividers have been used to split it into four identical shapes. You need to do the same for the two other puzzles below.

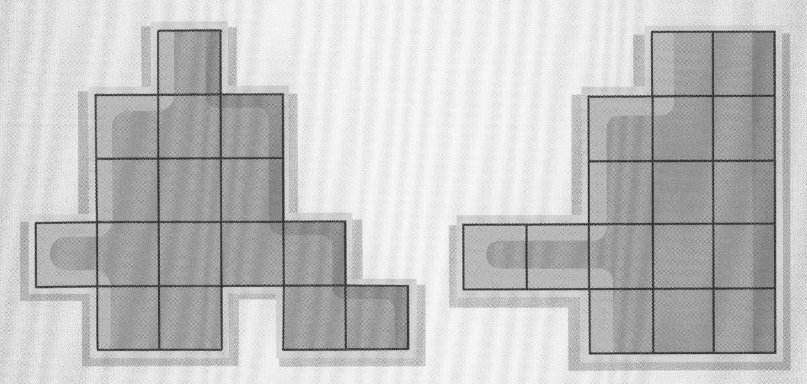

Divide each of the two puzzles so that they are split into four identical shapes. The shapes in each puzzle may be rotated relative to each other.

As you place the last divider into the panel, a secret passageway is revealed.

ANUBIS'S MAZE

You run up the passageway and emerge into a vast cavern within the pyramid. Right in front of you is a stone plinth with a maze drawn on it:

OVER-AND-UNDER MAZE

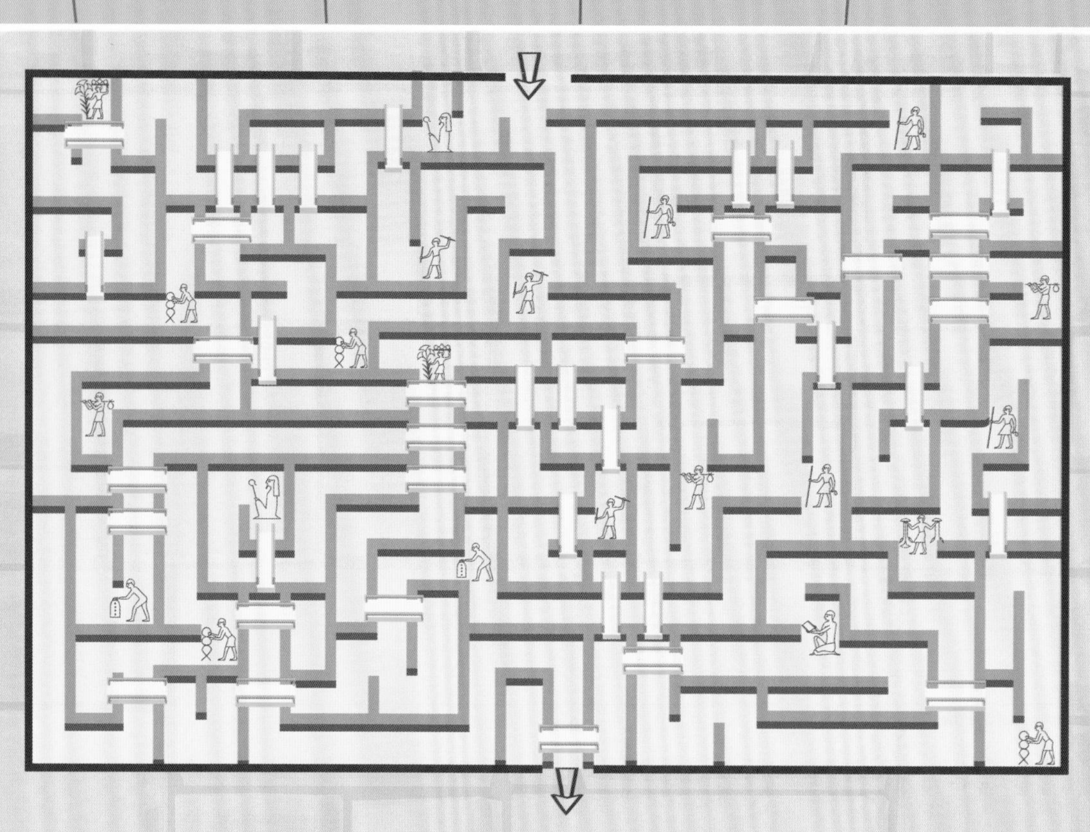

Beneath the maze is written

WHAT WILL IT COST YOU TO ESCAPE?

Can you answer this question?

Find a way through the maze from the entrance arrow at the top to the exit arrow at the bottom. Some paths cross over others using bridges. You can also travel underneath the bridges. Once you have found the most direct route from entrance to exit, can you work out the total value of the hieroglyphs on that route?

THE RIDDLES OF ANUBIS

You state the total value out loud and are surprised to hear a ghostly voice speaking from a statue of Anubis that stands within the room:

TWO GODS KNOW I, BUT FROM ONE I SHOULD FLY.

ONE GOD TELLS THE TRUTH. THE OTHER WILL LIE.

IF I ASK ONE A QUESTION, WHAT SHOULD IT BE?

I WISH TO KNOW FROM WHICH I SHOULD FLEE!

There are two Egyptian gods. One will always tell the truth. The other will always lie. You don't know which is which, and you only get one question—so the question has to work for either god!

What should that question be, so you can work out which god is which?

You tell Anubis your answer, and he responds:

ANOTHER GOD HAS JOINED US NOW. HE CAN SAY WHATEVER HE LIKES! IF ONE OF THE THREE GODS TELLS YOU, "I ALWAYS LIE," WHICH OF THE THREE GODS IS THAT? REMEMBER, ONE GOD LIES, ONE GOD TELLS THE TRUTH, AND ONE GOD CAN DO EITHER.

You give your answer out loud, and to your surprise the statue of Anubis comes to life and says,

"Follow me. . . ."

THE HIDDEN PATH

You follow Anubis along a path, and before long you come across a wall decorated with eight panels, each containing a cartouche made up of three hieroglyphs.

A cartouche is a group of hieroglyphs surrounded by a border. In ancient Egypt, they were used to represent royal names. In this book the word simply refers to a group of hieroglyphs.

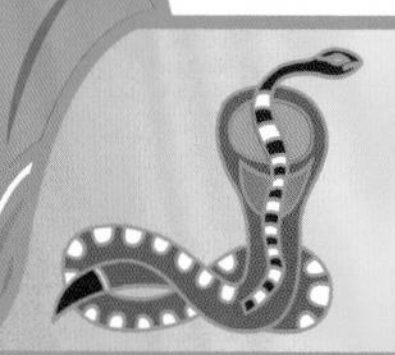

CARTOUCHE CONUNDRUM

The panels look like this:

Below is written:

Find the differences—on reflection!

Can you find the differences? Each cartouche contains exactly one difference in its reflected form, so you are looking for a total of four differences—one per row.

As you highlight the last difference with your finger, suddenly the wall splits in two down the center line and slides open, granting you access to a hidden bridge.

You step onto the bridge, which crosses a lily pond. Anubis blocks your exit from the bridge, demanding that you pass his test before you proceed.

You notice that each lily pad has a different number on it:

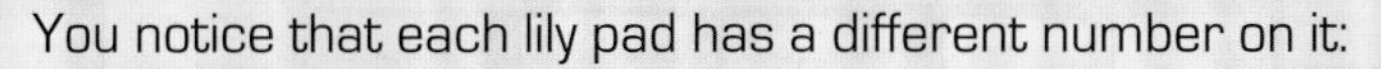

LILY POND PUZZLE

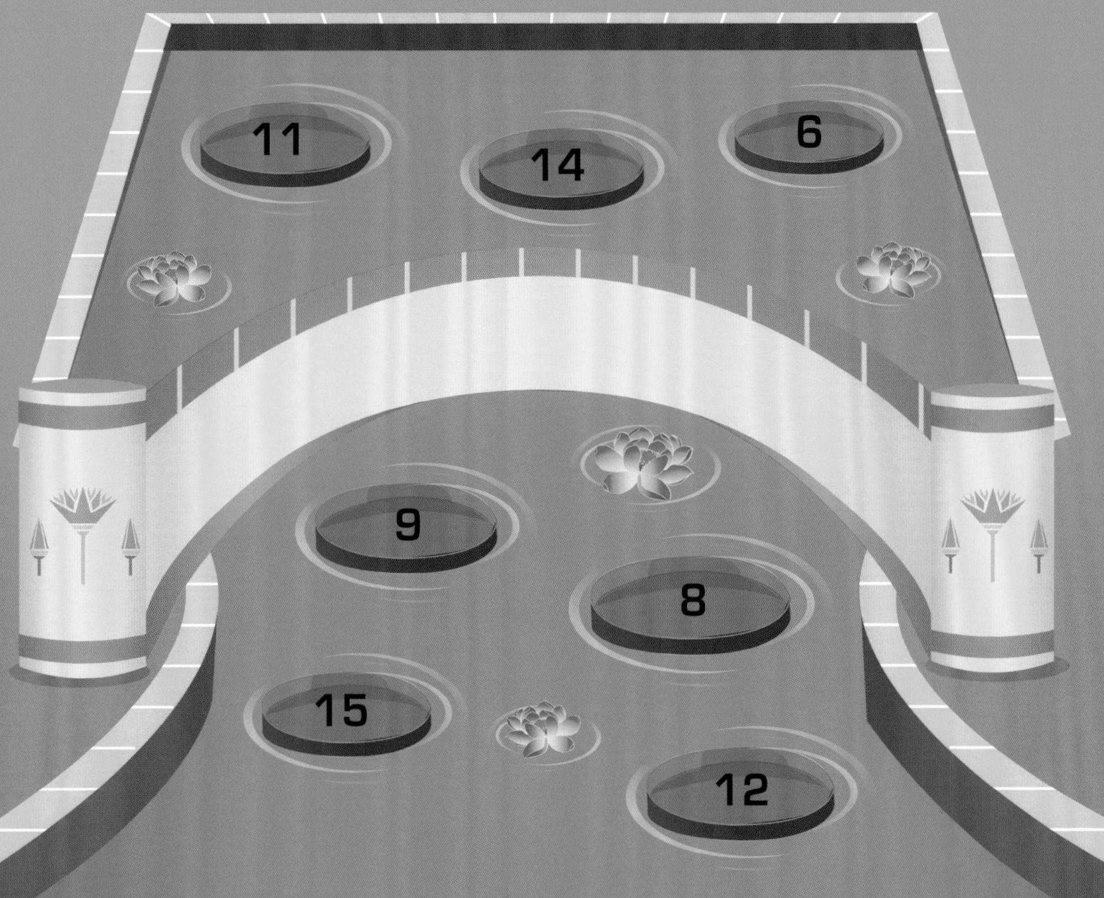

Which lily pads add up to each of these totals?

30 39 45 53

For example, to reach a total of 24 you would choose the 9 and 15 lily pads since 24 = 9 +15. Can you find the correct set of lily pads for each of the totals?

Anubis is pleased with your answers and steps off the bridge, commanding you to follow him.

A PAPYRUS PUZZLE

Anubis vanishes into a cave, but by the time you follow him inside, he is nowhere to be seen.

The cave is roughly hewn, with flaming torches mounted along the walls. In the center of the cave is a stone table with some sheets of papyrus. Each sheet has delicately inked hieroglyphs written on it. The writing is slightly faded but is still clear, and the first sheet you pick up looks like this:

WHERE IS THE TREASURE?

Anubis's ghostly voice whispers from somewhere out of sight:

Find my unique treasure, and I will help you find your way.

He seems to be asking you to find something unique—does that help?

Work out what the text means and identify the appropriate hieroglyph.

THE HIDDEN SYMBOLS

You pick up a second sheet, which looks somewhat different, with neatly ruled lines and a highlighted region in the center of the papyrus.

On the back of the papyrus are eight cartouches.

One of these eight sets of symbols fits into the highlighted center section. Can you work out which one?

In a correctly completed grid, no hieroglyph repeats in any row or column, and identical hieroglyphs don't touch—not even diagonally.

You sketch out the solution in the loose sand of the cave, and the sound of falling rock draws your attention to the far end of the cave. A small opening has appeared.

LET'S GET OUT OF HERE

You walk over to the newly revealed opening, where a large and elaborate panel is now clearly visible. It looks like this:

THE HIDDEN EXIT ROUTE

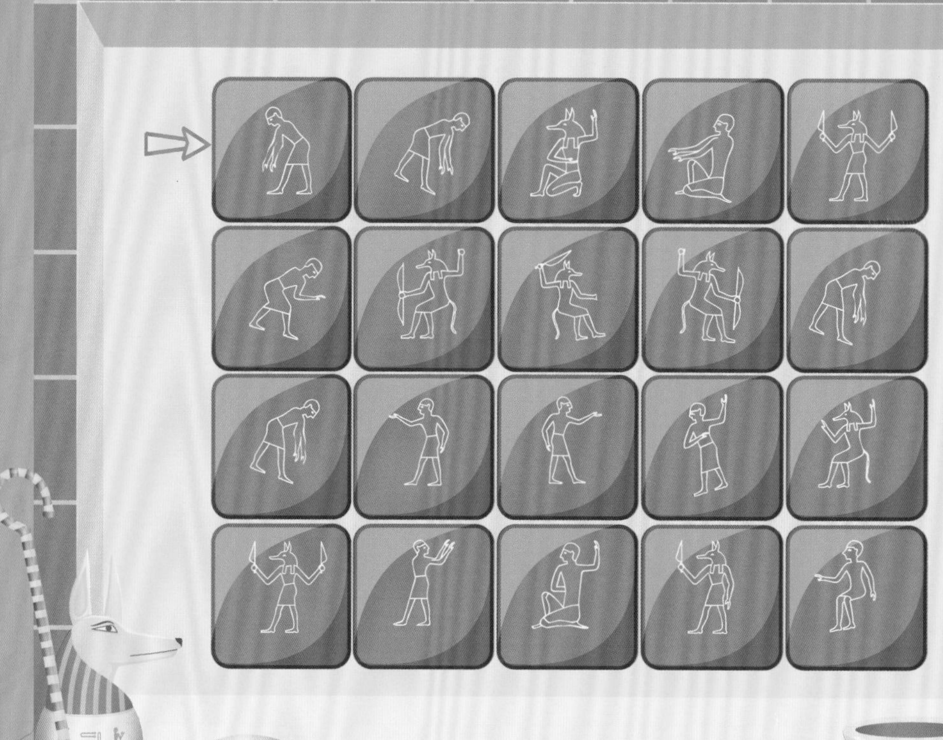

Beneath it is written a brief message:

THE ENTRANCE IS MARKED WITH AN ARROW, BUT WHERE WILL YOU EXIT? LET ONLY HUMANS BE YOUR GUIDE!

Start at the square marked with an arrow and trace a route to the hidden exit.

THE SANDS OF TIME

You trace the hidden exit route, and the panel comes crashing down, revealing an even deeper part of the hidden opening. Inside are two sand timers.

Each timer has a different number on it and is filled with sand. When you turn each timer over, the sand flows slowly from the top to the bottom and takes as many minutes to run all the way through as the number marked on it. This means that the "3" timer will time three minutes, and the "5" timer will time five minutes.

Anubis appears and challenges you to work out how to time exactly SEVEN minutes, using just these two sand timers. You need to find a way to do it precisely, without guessing!

You puzzle out a clever method and successfully time seven minutes. As your reward, Anubis reveals a stone staircase that leads up to daylight.

THE FINAL GATE

At the top of the stairs, your final task awaits!

A gate is locked shut with a set of numeric padlocks. You need to solve a clue to work out the correct number to open each padlock. Then, and only then, you can escape from the pyramid into the daylight outside!

PADLOCKS

1 How many steps did you take to cross the floor tiles when avoiding the snakes?

2 Which number was never hit by any arrow in the room of arrow traps?

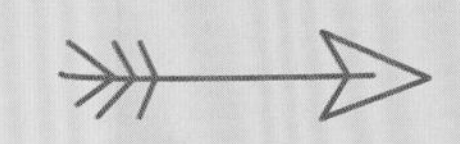

3 What was the value of this symbol in the room beneath the canopic jars?

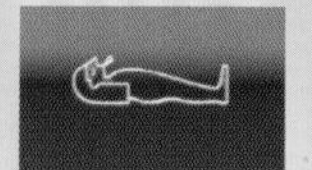

4 What was the total of the hieroglyphs you didn't visit on your route through the maze on the stone plinth?

5 There is one hieroglyph that appears more than any other on the first papyrus you found in the cave. How many oars are there on that hieroglyph?

6 How many creatures did you pass over and ignore when finding the exit point on the elaborate wall panel?

You will need to turn back to earlier pages to find the answers to the questions and remember your solutions to previous puzzles!

Eventually you enter the correct number into each padlock, and as you unlock the sixth one successfully, you hurriedly push the door open and clamber quickly up the remaining steps and out of the pyramid.

ESCAPE

You step out into the glaring hot sun of the desert and are greeted by a train of camels. You are pleased that the sandstorm is long gone.

The next day you return with friends to show them the amazing pyramid that you explored. But both the entrance and exit are now gone. The wind and the desert have reclaimed their secrets.

Perhaps it will be a few thousand years more before anyone else can repeat your incredible journey. . . .

PYRAMID PUZZLES HINTS

Not sure how to solve a puzzle? Use these hints to help.

Each puzzle has a series of numbered hints. Read hint 1 first, and see if it helps. Then only read each further hint if you still need it—the hints will become more and more specific about how to solve the puzzle.

PAGES 6–7

INSTALLING TORCHES

1. Match the shapes at the bottom of each torch with the holder indents above.
2. For example, torch E fits into holder 3.

PAGES 6–7

LIGHTING THE WAY 1

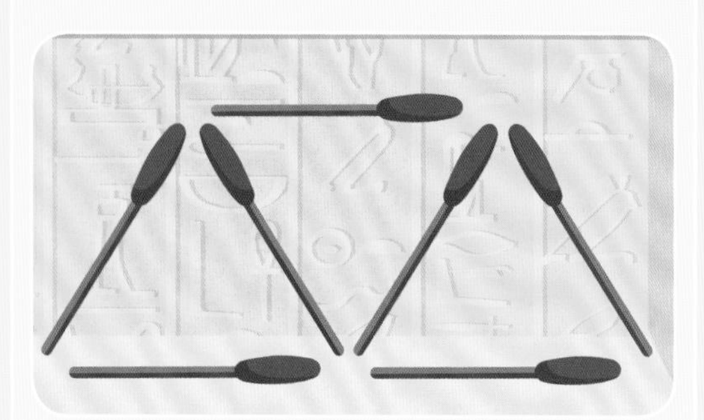

1. These three triangles are all the same size, but the two you will make won't be the same size.
2. You need to nest a smaller triangle inside a larger outer triangle.

PAGES 6–7

LIGHTING THE WAY 2

1. You need to place the smaller triangle of matches inside the larger triangle in some way.
2. The triangle count includes the larger triangle that's already made, plus a number of smaller ones.

PAGES 8–9

ACROSS THE TILED FLOOR

1. The first two moves both use the same hieroglyph, so you will move a certain number of squares down, and then the same number of squares to the right.
2. The first move can't be 1 down because the following 1 right would hit a snake. It can't be more than 2 either because that would hit a snake right away, so the first hieroglyph must be a 2.
3. There are no up arrows, so the numbers moving down must add up to 9.
4. You can already see that two of the down moves are 2s, which accounts for 4 (2+2) squares downward. There are three other down moves, which must sum to 5. This means that the hieroglyph that appears twice, the sitting Egyptian, must be a 1, and the other hieroglyph used to move downward, with the three circles, must be a 3.
5. Now you can more easily work out which is 4, which is 5, and which is 6.

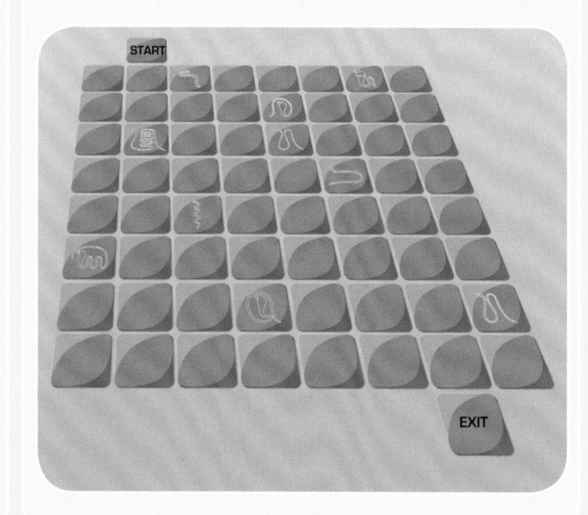

PAGES 8–9

THE SEALED DOOR

1. Use the hieroglyph values from the previous puzzle. Copy out the grids exactly but convert the hieroglyphs to numbers.
2. On the right-hand side of the top puzzle, the snake must travel up two squares due to the shaded squares. On the left-hand side of the same puzzle, the 1 clue at the top is already fulfilled, so the snake must travel to the right from this point. This gets you this far:

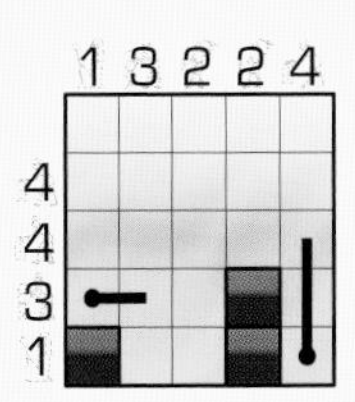

3. At this point, the 3 in the second-last row and the 1 in the bottom row are already solved, so the snake must go up on the left-hand side. And in the rightmost column, the only way to fulfill the 4 clue is if the snake goes up again and turns left:

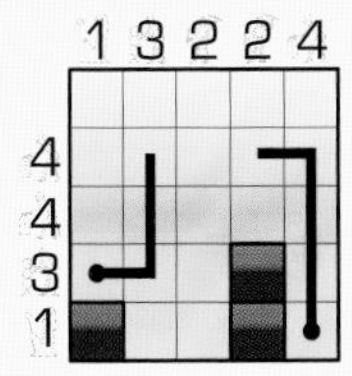

4. You can now use similar logic, plus various guesses, to connect the two dots and find the hidden snake!
5. For the second puzzle, start by working out how the snake must be placed in the top row, and then continue from there.

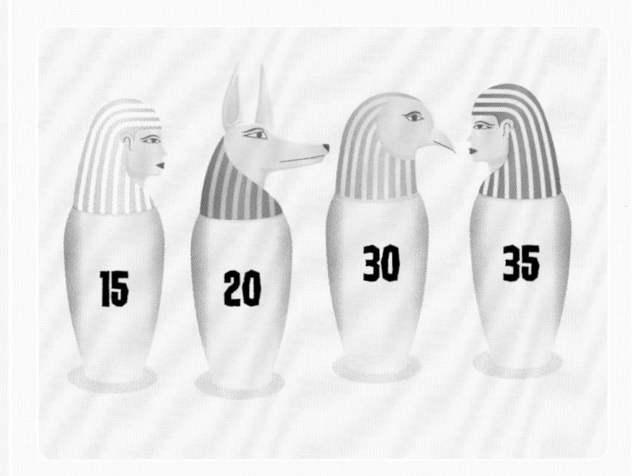

PAGES 10–11

THE ROOM OF ARROWS

1. The solution to 20 uses the 3 on the first door.
2. The solution to 30 uses the 12 on the first door.

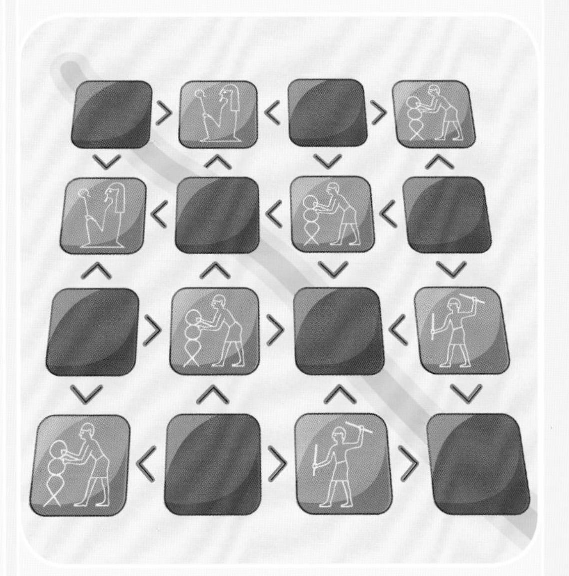

PAGES 10–11

ARROW HIEROGLYPHS

1. Use the value of the hieroglyphs you worked out for the tiled floor puzzle.
2. As a hint, tiles don't repeat in a row or column. This makes it much easier!
3. If a tile is less than some neighbors but greater than others, it must be a 2 or 3.

PAGES 12–13
THE MUMMY'S CHAMBER 1

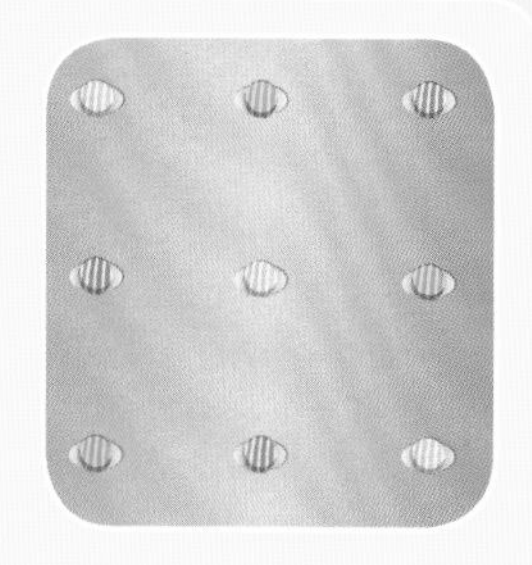

1. Some of the lines that make up your path will need to expand outside the boundaries of the nine jars.

PAGES 12–13
THE MUMMY'S CHAMBER 2

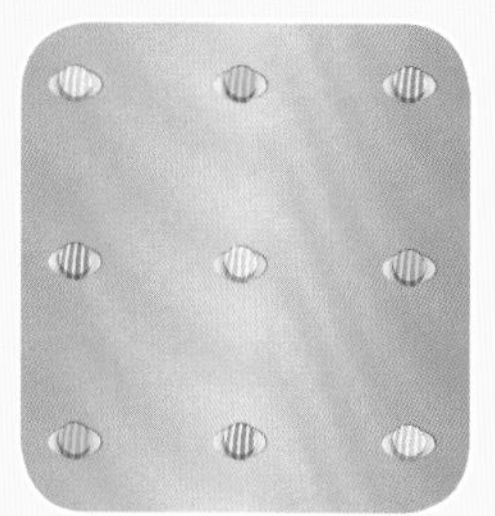

1. Draw an outer square.
2. Then draw a second square to make five areas.
3. The final result has both horizontal and vertical symmetry.

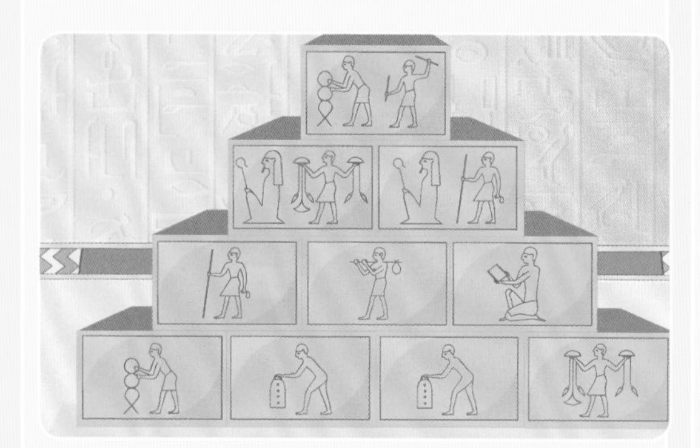

PAGES 14–15
A PYRAMID MYSTERY

1. Use the hieroglyphs for 1 to 6 from previous puzzles.
2. Use the completed pyramid to work out what 7, 8, and 9 look like.
3. The unknown hieroglyph in the second pyramid is 0.
4. Copy out the incomplete pyramid, converting the hieroglyphs to numbers. Starting with the top block's value, subtract the value of the block you already know directly below. The result must be the value of the unknown block in the second row down.
5. Work out the value of every block and convert back to hieroglyphs to work out which tile goes where.

PAGES 14–15
A SECRET PANEL

1. Count how many tiles are in each of the bottom puzzles and work out how many tiles will be in each of the four shapes.
2. There are four tiles in each of the four shapes.
3. Start with the sticking-out area at the bottom-right of the left-hand puzzle. This tells you what each of the shapes in this puzzle looks like.

PAGES 16–17
OVER-AND-UNDER MAZE

1. Use the hieroglyph values from previous puzzles.
2. There is only one solution to the maze.

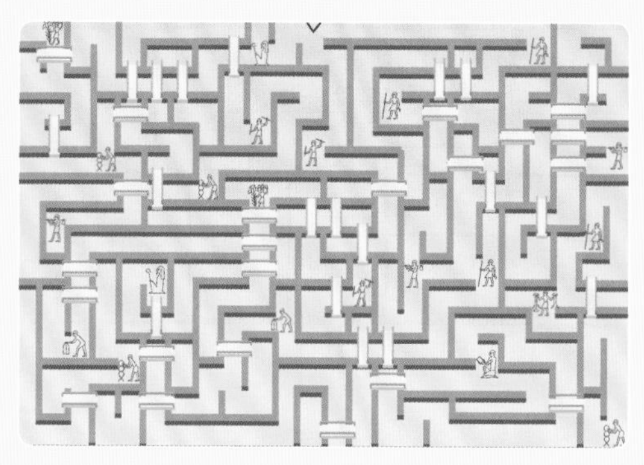

PAGES 16–17
THE RIDDLES OF ANUBIS 1

1. Ask a question for which both gods would give the same answer.
2. You will need to ask one god what the other god would say since in this way you will get truth+lie or lie+truth. So with the right question, you'll get the same answer no matter which god you ask.
3. Then you just need to work out what that answer means!

PAGES 16–17
THE RIDDLES OHF ANUBIS 2

1. It can't be the god who always tells the truth since he couldn't say he always lies.
2. What about the lying god? Could he say this?
3. So which god is it?

PAGES 18–19

CARTOUCHE CONUNDRUM

1. In the first row, look at the bird of prey.

PAGES 18–19

LILY POND PUZZLE

1. You will need three or more numbers for each total.

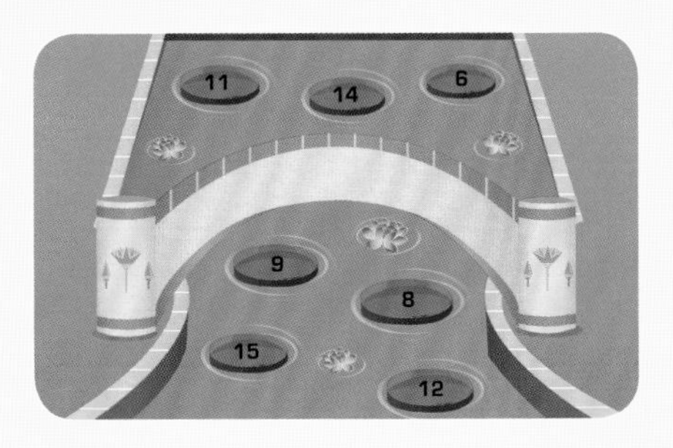

PAGES 20–21

WHERE IS THE TREASURE?

1. You are looking for the hieroglyph that only appears once.

PAGES 20–21

THE HIDDEN SYMBOLS

1. Eliminate options that would place identical hieroglyphs in the same row or column or diagonally next to one another.

PAGES 22–23

THE HIDDEN EXIT ROUTE

1. Each picture points in a particular direction.
2. Go in the direction pointed at each step, starting from the entrance square at the top left.
3. Skip over any square that doesn't have a human figure on it. Only obey the humans!

PAGES 22–23

THE SANDS OF TIME

1. You need to turn over one of the sand timers before it has finished. You don't do this by guessing but based on when the other sand timer finishes.
2. Doing this, you can time an amount of two minutes by using the 3-minute timer in a certain way. You then add this to the 5-minute timer for a total of seven minutes.

PAGES 24–25

PADLOCKS

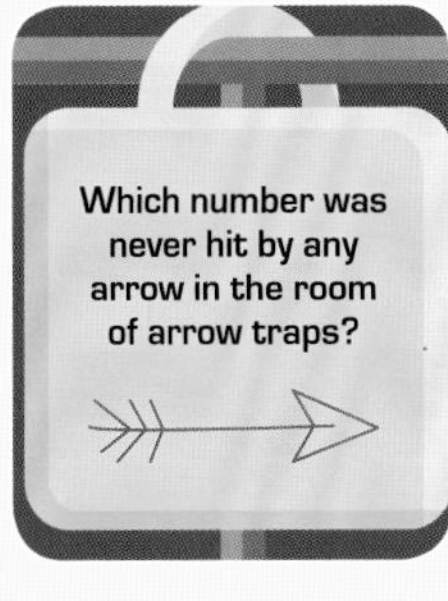

1. Padlock 1
   Refer back to page 8 or check the solution if you can't remember how you did it!
2. Padlock 2
   Did you notice that one of the numbers was never used in the puzzle on page 10? Which one was it?
3. Padlock 3
   You had to work out the value of this symbol using a process of elimination. What was it?
4. Padlock 4
   Add up all the hieroglyphs on page 16, then subtract the total you found before. This will result in the total of the remaining hieroglyphs.
5. Padlock 5
   One hieroglyph appears four times on page 20. It has oars—how many oars does it have?
6. Padlock 6
   Retrace your route and count how many nonhuman squares you pass over while following that route. That's your answer.

PYRAMID PUZZLES SOLUTIONS

PAGES 6–7
INSTALLING TORCHES

The torch and holder pairs are A5, B4, C2, D1, and E3.

PAGES 6–7
LIGHTING THE WAY

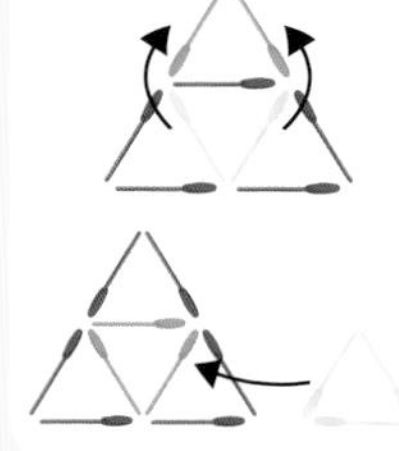

PAGES 8–9
ACROSS THE TILED FLOOR

This means that the hieroglyphs have the following values:

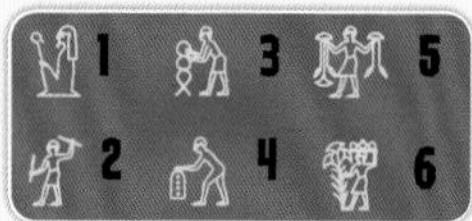

PAGES 8–9
THE SEALED DOOR

The solutions are as follows:

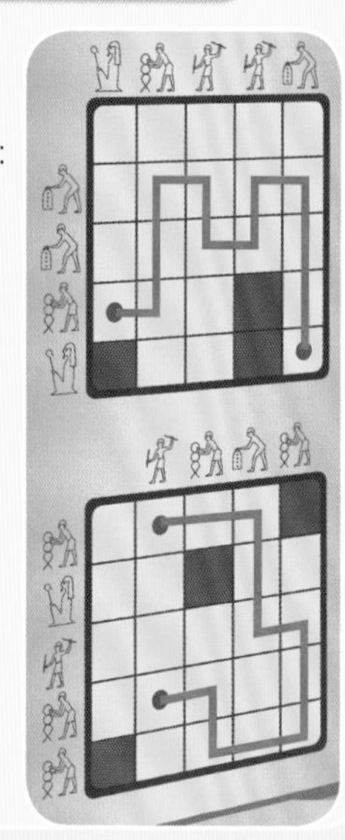

PAGES 10–11
THE ROOM OF ARROWS

15 = 3 + 5 + 7
20 = 3 + 10 + 7
30 = 12 + 10 + 8
35 = 12 + 14 + 9

PAGES 10–11
ARROW HIEROGLYPHS

Exchanging hieroglyphs for digits and then solving the puzzle results in the following:

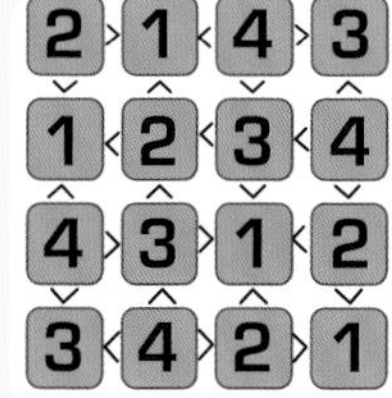

So the solution is:

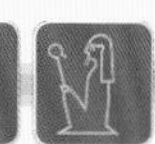

PAGES 12–13
THE MUMMY'S CHAMBER

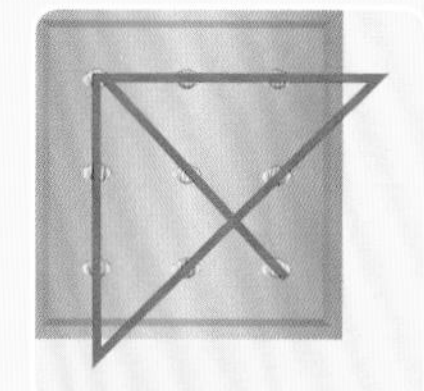
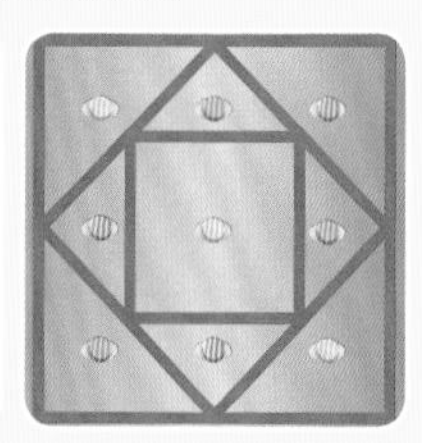

PAGES 14–15
A PYRAMID MYSTERY

The four new hieroglyphs are:

PAGES 14–15
A SECRET PANEL

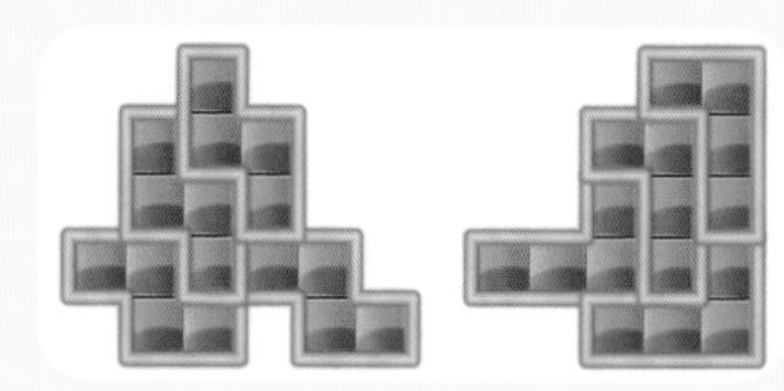

PAGES 16–17

OVER-AND-UNDER MAZE

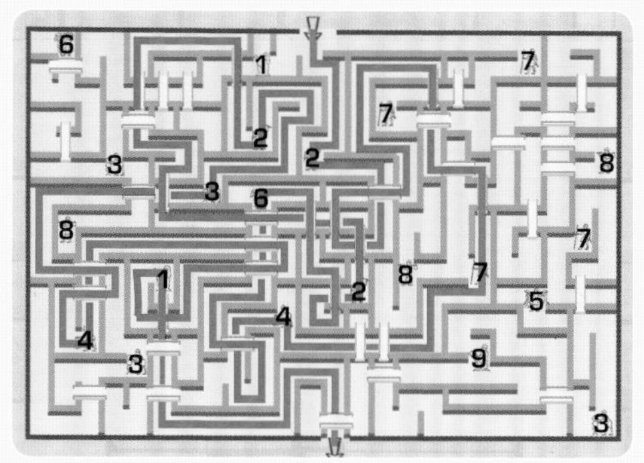

The total value of the route through the maze is therefore 2+7+4+6+2+2+3+4+1 = 31. All other paths lead to dead ends.

PAGES 16–17

THE RIDDLES OF ANUBIS

RIDDLE 1:

Ask one of the gods, “Which god would the other god say tells the truth?” Whichever god is given as the answer will be the god who always lies. The other god will be the one who always tells the truth. Try it out, and you’ll see that this always works!

RIDDLE 2:

The truth-telling god can’t say “I always lie” since that wouldn’t be true. The lie-telling god can’t say “I always lie” because it would be true, and not a lie! **So it must be the third god that just joined.**

PAGES 18–19

CARTOUCHE CONUNDRUM

PAGES 18–19

LILY POND PUZZLE

30 = 6+9+15; 39 = 6+8+11+14;
45 = 8+11+12+14; 53 = 6+9+11+12+15

PAGES 20–21

WHERE IS THE TREASURE?

This hieroglyph only appears once:

PAGES 20–21

THE HIDDEN SYMBOLS

PAGES 22–23

THE HIDDEN EXIT ROUTE

Follow the path that the human characters point at, but ignore the nonhuman characters. The exit is downward from the bottom-left tile:

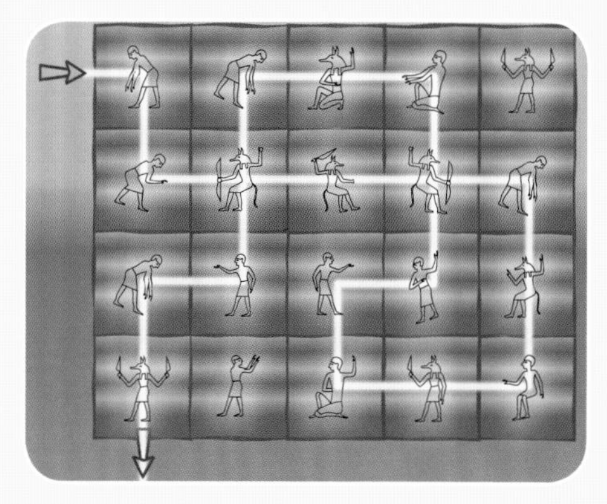

PAGES 22–23

THE SANDS OF TIME

Turn both timers over. When the 3-minute one finishes, turn it over again. Now when the 5-minute one finishes, you are only two minutes into the time of the 3-minute one. So now turn the 3-minute one back over again, even though it hasn’t finished, to time those two minutes again. Once this finishes, you’re done!

PAGES 24–25

PADLOCKS

Padlock 1 = 26 steps
Padlock 2 = 15
Padlock 3 = 0
Padlock 4 = 75
Padlock 5 = The hieroglyph is
so the answer is 2. (Or 1 will open the padlock too since it isn’t clear if that really is an oar hidden behind the boat.)
Padlock 6 = 9

INDEX

THE AUTHOR

Dr. Gareth Moore is the author of a wide range of puzzle and brain-training books for both children and adults, including *The Kids' Book of Puzzles, The Mammoth Book of Brain Games,* and *The Rough Guide Book of Brain Training.* He is also the founder of the daily brain training website www.BrainedUp.com. He gained his PhD from Cambridge University (UK) in the field of computer speech recognition, teaching machines to understand spoken words.